Poems from the Greek Anthology

POEMS FROM THE GREEK ANTHOLOGY

Translated, with a Foreword, by KENNETH REXROTH
with drawings by Geraldine Sakall

Ann Arbor Paperbacks   The University of Michigan Press

Designed by George Lenox
Second printing 1967
First edition as an Ann Arbor Paperback 1962
Copyright © by The University of Michigan 1962
All rights reserved
Published in the United States of America by
The University of Michigan Press and simultaneously
in Rexdale, Canada, by Ambassador Books Limited
Library of Congress Catalog Card No. 62-9691
Manufactured in the United States of America

For my friend—
James Laughlin
Halicarnassian host and guest

Go tell the King: The daedal
Walls have fallen to the earth
Phoibos has no sanctuary,
No prophetic laurel, no
Speaking spring. The garrulous
Water has dried up at last.

THE LAST UTTERANCE OF THE DELPHIC ORACLE

Foreword

It is with great reluctance that I give this book to the press. The first translation from the Greek I ever did was the Apple Orchard of Sappho in my fifteenth year. It left me so excited with accomplishment that I couldn't sleep well for nights. Since that time, on the freight trains of my youthful years of wandering, in starlit camps on desert and mountain ranges, in snow-covered cabins, on shipboard, in bed, in the bath, in love, in times of loneliness and despair, in jail, while employed as an attendant of the insane, and on many other jobs and in many other places, the *Anthology* and the lyric poets of Greece have been my constant companions. They, and the Chinese, have shaped me for better or worse as a poet, and they have given me whatever philosophy of life I have—along with life itself.

Now they are moving away from me to the printed page and I will miss them terribly.

As translations, these poems make no pretense of scholarship. Some are quite literal, others are so free as to be ironic comments on the Greek text. I have used various editions at various times, mostly the Didot, the Teubner, the Loeb. Many of the translations came to me as I turned the Greek poem over in memory, with no text at all.

Along with the epigrams of the *Anthology* are a few lyric fragments and some bits of Latin. Once I thought I might do a book from the Latin Anthology, the Petroniana, Luxorius, Maximian's Fifth Elegy, Amare Liceat, Martial, Ausonius, some of the *Carmina Burana*, and the Plaints of Abelard. Actually

Latin verse, with its rhetorical emphasis, does not interest me greatly, and it is unlikely that now I shall ever devote so much time to it. So these few pieces are scattered amongst the 100 Poems from the *Greek Anthology* as an extra dividend.

I have provided no notes or other apparatus—the last word of scholarship on these things has been said long ago—and the poems themselves need no explications. In a few cases, what might seem to the pedants to be mistranslations are deliberate *jeux d'esprit*. I know what the Greek says. After much thought I decided to transliterate the Greek proper names directly, rather than in their Latinized forms.

K. R.

Poems from the Greek Anthology

Restless and discontent
I lie awake all night long.
And as I drowse in the dawn,
The swallows stir in the eaves,
And wake me weeping again.
I press my eyes close tight, but
Your face rises before me.
O birds, be quiet with
Your tittering accusations.
I did not cut that dead girl's tongue.
Go weep for her lover in the hills,
Cry by the hoopoe's nest in the rocks.
Let me sleep for a while, and dream
I lie once more in my girl's arms.

AGATHIAS SCHOLASTICOS

Dawn after dawn comes on the wine
Spilt on the books and music,
And on the stained and tumbled pillows.
And then, while we are paying
No attention, a black man comes,
And roasts some of us, and fries
Some of us, and boils some of us,
And throws us all in the dump.

AMMIANOS

It is necessary that things
Should pass away into that from
Which they were born.
All things must pay
To each other the penalties
And compensations for all the
Inequalities wrought by time.

ANIXAMANDROS

4

Among the dead we come
To great Demeter, nine
Of us, all virgins, each
Of us dressed in lovely
Robes, dressed in lovely robes,
And each of us with a
Splendid necklace of
Lustrous carved ivory.

ANONYMOUS FRAGMENT

Awake all night till the
Beautiful morning star,
Leontion lay, taking
Her full of golden Sthenios.
Now she offers to Kypris
The lyre she played with the
Muses, all through the long night,
On that night-long festival.

ANONYMOUS

Flowers will do us no good on our tombstones;
Tears mixed with ashes only make mud.
Let's move half the garden into the bedroom,
Roll about, and moan in unison.

ANONYMOUS

I grew from the earth.
I flourished in my day.
I am earth again.
My name was Aristokles,
The son of Menon,
A citizen of the Peiraieus.

ANONYMOUS TOMB

I have two sicknesses, Love
And Poverty. Poverty
I can stand, but the fever
Of Love is unbearable.

ANONYMOUS

I keep the taste of feasting,
And the wage of wantonness,
And the joys shared with lovers;
But the blessings of many
Possessions I leave behind.

ANONYMOUS

I know I am poor,
Neither do I have to be reminded
Of my own name or
The day of the week.
All your bitterness will get us nowhere.
Wash the anchovies,
While I pour the wine.
Naked and drunk, we'll find riches in bed.

ANONYMOUS

Oh! What is the matter?
Please be quiet. Get up
And go before he comes
Or he will do something
Terrible to you and
Worse to me. It is dawn
Already. Can't you see
The light through the window?

ANONYMOUS EARLY GREEK FOLKSONG

O restless, caressing eyes,
You say a certain special thing.
Pleasure and light love sit there,
And sensuousness sits between.

ANONYMOUS

This little stone, dear Sabinos,
Is all the memorial
Of our great love. I miss you
Always, and I hope that you
Did not drink forgetfulness
Of me when you drank the waters
Of death with the new dead.

ANONYMOUS
A GRAVESTONE AT CORINTH

With your beautiful hair and seemly
Years and candid face, sweetly,
As I lay still, you gave me
Caressing kisses. If now I never
May see you waking, I hope sleep
Holds my eyes bound shut forever.

ANONYMOUS

I am constantly wounded
By the deadly gossip that adds
Insult to injury, that
Punishes me mercilessly
With the news of your latest
Scandal in my ears. Wherever
I go the smirking fame of each
Fresh despicable infamy
Has run on ahead of me.
Can't you learn to be cautious
About your lecheries?
Hide your practices in darkness;
Keep away from raised eyebrows.
If you must murder love, do it
Covertly, with your candied
Prurience and murmured lewdness.

You were never the heroine
Of dirty stories in the days
When love bound us together.
Now those links are broken, desire
Is frozen, and you are free
To indulge every morbid lust,
And filthy jokes about your
Latest amour are the delight
Of every cocktail party.

Your boudoir is a brothel;
Your salon is a saloon;
Even your sensibilities
And your depraved innocence
Are only special premiums,
Rewards of a shameful commerce.

O the heart breaking memory
Of days like flowers, and your
Eyes that shone like Venus the star
In our brief nights, and the soft bird
Flight of your love about me;
And now your eyes are as bitter
As a rattlesnake's dead eyes,
And your disdain as malignant.
Those who give off the smell of coin
You warm in bed; I who have
Love to bring am not even
Allowed to speak to you now.
You receive charlatans and fools;
I have only the swindling
Memory of poisoned honey.

ANONYMOUS
CARMINA BURANA
(ABELARD?)

Bitto gives to Athena
Her thrumming loom comb,
The tool of a poor living,
And says, "Hail, goddess, take it back.
A widow of forty, I
Abandon your gifts, and turn
Instead to the business of
Love. Desire is stronger than age."

ANTIPATROS OF SIDON

Fortune-tellers say I won't last long;
It looks like it from the newspapers;
But there is better conversation
In Hell than in an insane nation;
And a galloping jug will get there
Quicker than these loud pedestrians,
Tumbling down hill witless in the dust.

ANTIPATROS

Never again, Orpheus
Will you lead the enchanted oaks,
Nor the rocks, nor the beasts
That are their own masters.
Never again will you sing to sleep
The roaring wind, nor the hail,
Nor the drifting snow, nor the boom
Of the sea wave.
You are dead now.
Led by your mother, Calliope,
The Muses shed many tears
Over you for a long time.
What good does it do us to mourn
For our sons when the immortal
Gods are powerless to save
Their own children from death?

ANTIPATROS

Where is your famous beauty,
Corinth of the Dorians?
Where is your crown of towers?
Where are your ancient treasures?
Where are the temples of the
Immortals, and where are the
Houses and the wives of the
Lineage of Sisyphos,
All your myriad people?
Most unhappy city, not
A trace is left of you. War
Has seized and eaten it all.
Only the inviolate
Sea nymphs, the daughters of the
Ocean, remain, crying like
Sea birds over your sorrows.

ANTIPATROS

Neither war, nor cyclones, nor earthquakes
Are as terrifying as this oaf,
Who stares, sips water, and remembers
Everything we say.

ANTIPATROS OF THESSALONIKA

I, Hermes, have been set up
Where three roads cross, by the windy
Orchard above the grey beach.
Here tired men may rest from travel,
By my cold, clean, whispering spring.

ANYTE

Kypris keeps this spot.
She loves to be here,
Always looking out
From the land over
The brilliant sea. She
Brings the sailors good
Voyage, and the sea
Quivers in awe of
Her gleaming image.

ANYTE

The children have put purple
Reins on you, he goat, and a
Bridle in your bearded mouth.
And they play at horse races
Round a temple where a god
Gazes on their childish joy.

ANYTE

Will, lost in a sea of trouble,
Rise, save yourself from the whirlpool
Of the enemies of willing.
Courage exposes ambushes.
Steadfastness destroys enemies.
Keep your victories hidden.
Do not sulk over defeat.
Accept good. Bend before evil.
Learn the rhythm which binds all men.

ARCHILOCHOS

The sun will never see you
Again, singing your shrill tune,
In the fine home Alkis gave
You. You have flown away to
The meadows of Pluto and
The dew drenched flowers of
Golden Persephone.

ARISTODIKOS OF RHODES

Although she's a girl, Dorkion
Is wise to the ways of the boys.
Like a chubby kid, she knows how
To throw over her shoulder, from
Under her broadbrimmed hat, the quick
Glance of Public Love, and let her
Cape show a glimpse of her bare butt.

ASKLEPIADES OF SAMOS

Didyme waved her wand at me.
I am utterly enchanted.
The sight of her beauty makes me
Melt like wax before the fire. What
Is the difference if she is black?
So is coal, but alight, it shines like roses.

ASKLEPIADES

Get drunk, my boy, don't weep, you're
Not the only prisoner
Of love. Plenty of people
Are stuck all over with the
Barbed arrows of lust. Don't
Grovel. You're still alive.
Drink your liquor straight. Drink. Time
Is wasting. We may not be
Here at bedtime. Drink. Soon
Enough and long enough,
You'll find time for sleeping.

ASKLEPIADES

It is sweet in summer to slake
Your thirst with snow, and the spring breeze
Is sweet to the sailors after
The stormy winter, but sweetest
Of all when one blanket hides two
Lovers at the worship of Kypris.

ASKLEPIADES

Love has found out how to mix
Beauty with beauty. Not
Emerald with gold, which does not
Gleam and sparkle like these do,
Nor ivory with ebony,
Less dark and light than these are,
But Kleandros and Eubotis—
Flowers of Love and Persuasion.

ASKLEPIADES

Lysidike dedicates
To you, Kypris, her jockey's
Spur, the golden prickle she
Wore on her beautiful leg.
Upside down, she broke many
Horses, yet her own bottom
Was never reddened, she had
Such a skillful seat that she
Always came first in the race.
Now she hangs her weapon in
The midst of your golden gate.

ASKLEPIADES

Playing once with facile
Hermione, I found she wore
A flower embroidered girdle
And on it, in letters of gold,
"Love me, and never mind
If others had me before you."

ASKLEPIADES

Snow! Hail! Lower! Lightning! Thunder!
Go ahead. Empty your black clouds
On the earth. If you kill me, I
Will give up, but if I live, I
Can stand worse than this and still sing
Before her door. I am the slave
Of a god who is your master
Too; remember, once he turned you
To gold and drove you through walls of brass.

ASKLEPIADES

What are you saving it for?
When you get to Hell you'll find
Nobody there to love you, girl.
The fun of love is for the
Living. Dead virgins are just
Dust and ashes like us all.

ASKLEPIADES

I used to tell you, "Frances, we grow old.
The years fly away. Don't be so private
With those parts. A chaste maid is an old maid."
Unnoticed by your disdain, old age crept
Close to us. Those days are gone past recall.
And now you come, penitent and crying
Over your old lack of courage, over
Your present lack of beauty. It's all right.
Closed in your arms, we'll share our smashed delights.
It's give and take now. It's what I wanted,
If not what I want.

AUSONIUS, after RUFINUS

Your flatteries are boring,
And your coquetries painful.
I am not godlike, and I
Am extremely impatient.
I am not going to turn
Into a bull or a swan,
Let alone a bufflehead,
Like cuckold Amphitryon.
Take off your clothes and lie down,
Or I shall get me a girl
Who wants a human lover.

BASSOS

I am not going to turn into gold,
And let somebody else become a bull,
Or sing like a swan along the shore.
Such stunts I leave to Zeus.
Instead of becoming a bird,
I give Corinna two dollars.

BASSOS

The lines are cast and the nets are set and waiting.
Now the tunnies come, slipping through the moonlit water.

THE DELPHIC ORACLE

Nothing but laughter, nothing
But dust, nothing but nothing,
No reason why it happens.

GLYKON

Wine and treacherous proposals
Lulled Aglaonike to sleep,
And the lovemaking of Nikagoras
Was sweet. Here she dedicates
To Kypris the trophies of
Her deflowering, still heavy
With perfume, her sandals, the soft
Band that held her breasts, witnesses
Of her drowsiness and his violence.

HEDYLOS

In the Spring the quince and the
Pomegranate bloom in the
Sacred Park of the Maidens,
And the vine tendril curls in
The shade of the downy vine leaf.
But for me Love never sleeps.
He scorches me like a blaze
Of lightning and he shakes me
To the roots like a storm out of
Thrace, and he overwhelms my heart
With black frenzy and seasickness.

IBYKOS

You call that wine?
I call it mush.

THE EMPEROR JULIAN

Somebody told me you were dead,
Herakleitos, and I wept when
I remembered how many times
The sun had set as we gossiped
Together when you came to see
Me once from Halikarnassos.
Where are you now? Long, long ago
Ashes. But your "Nightingales" still
Live. Death snatches everything, but
He shall not lay his hand on them.

KALLIMACHOS

Time's fingers bend us slowly
With dubious craftsmanship,
That at last spoils all it forms.

KRATES

This torch, still burning in my hand,
Which I carried to victory,
Running swiftly in the sacred
Race of the young men,
A memorial of Prometheos
And the theft of fire,
I, Antiphanes,
The son of Antiphanes,
Dedicate to Hermes.

KRINAGORAS

A silver Love, an anklet,
Purple curls of her Lesbian
Hair, her translucent brassiere,
Her bronze mirror, the broad comb
Of boxwood that restrained her
Ringlets, Kallikleia hangs up
In the porch of faithful Kypris,
In thanks for her granted wish.

LEONIDAS OF TARENTUM

A staff and slippers hang here, Kypris,
Spoils won from Sochares the Cynic,
Along with his dirty oil flask,
His purse full of holes and the
Wisdom of the ages. They were
Hung among the garlands of your porch,
By beautiful Rhodon when he seduced
The white whiskered wiseacre.

LEONIDAS

A wallet, a rawhide goatskin, a cane,
A filthy oil flask, never cleaned out,
A penniless dog skin purse,
The hat which covered his cynical head,
These are the mementoes of Sochares
Flung into the tamarisk bush
By Famine when he died.

LEONIDAS

By themselves in the twilight
The cattle came home
Over the snow-drifted hill.
Profoundly asleep,
The cowboy lies by an oak,
Stricken by lightning.

LEONIDAS

Eileithyia, brought safe
Through the sharp pain of labor,
Lays at your glorious feet,
Ambrosia, her head bands,
And her gown, for in the tenth
Month she brought forth double fruit.

LEONIDAS

Evening and morning old Platthis kept
Away sleep and poverty, and in the gates
Of gray old age sang a tune to her
Spindle and distaff. Standing by her loom
In the dawn, she danced with the Graces
Over the long work of Pallas, or, lovely to see,
Smoothed the thread for the loom with her
Wrinkled hand on her withered knees.
At eighty years, beautiful Platthis,
The weaver of beauty, set eyes
On the waters of Acheron.

LEONIDAS

For that goatfucker, goatfooted
Pan, Teleso stretched this hide
On a plane tree, and in front
Of it hung up his well cut
Crook, smiter of bloody-eyed wolves,
His curdling buckets, and the leash
And collars of his keen-nosed pups.

LEONIDAS

Here is Klito's little shack.
Here is his little cornpatch.
Here is his tiny vineyard.
Here is his little woodlot.
Here Klito spent eighty years.

LEONIDAS

His poor mother gives Mikythos'
Picture to Bacchos. It is
Very badly painted. But
Bacchos, take care of Mikythos.
Even if the picture is
Worthless, it is all a poor
Woman can afford.

LEONIDAS

Philokles offers his bouncing
Ball to Hermes, along
With the other toys of his
Boyhood, his boxwood rattle,
The knuckle bones he once was
So crazy about, and his
Spinning top.

LEONIDAS

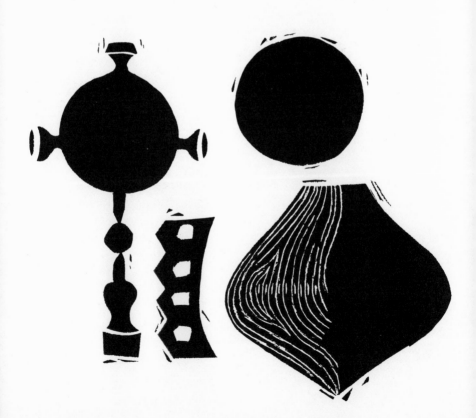

Theris, the old man who lived by his fish traps
And nets, more at home on the sea than a gull,
The terror of fishes, the net hauler, the prober
Of sea caves, who never sailed on a many oared ship,
Died in spite of Arcturus. No storm shipwrecked
His many decades. He died in his reed hut,
And went out by himself like a lamp at the
End of his years. No wife or child set up this
Tomb, but his fisherman's union.

LEONIDAS

Theris, whose hands were cunning,
Gives to Pallas, now the years
Of craftsmanship are over,
His stiff saw with curved handle,
His bright axe, his plane, and his
Revolving auger.

LEONIDAS

This beast which preyed on sheep
And cattle and herders alike, and
Which had no fear of barking dogs,
Eualkes of Crete killed in the night,
While guarding his herds, and hung up
For a trophy on this pine tree.

LEONIDAS

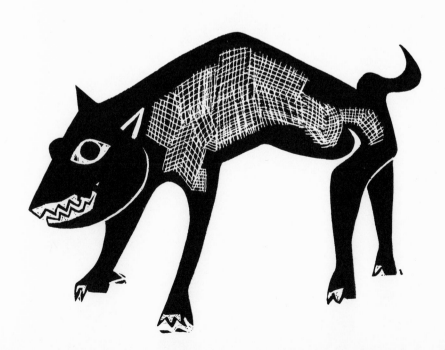

Traveler in the wilds, do not
Drink this roiled, muddy, warm water,
But go on over the hill where
The cows are grazing, and by the
Shepherds' pine you will find a
Murmuring spring, flowing from the
Rock, cold as snow on the North Wind.

LEONIDAS

For Glaukos, for the Nereids,
For Melekertes, the son of Ino,
For the gods of Samothrace,
And for all the submarine
Children of Chronos,
I, Lukillios, have cut off my hair.
Saved from the waves,
It is all I have left to offer.

LUCIAN

Dead, they'll burn you up with electricity,
An interesting experience,
But quite briefly illuminating—
So pour the whiskey and kiss my wife or yours,
And I'll reciprocate. Stop fretting your brains.
In Hell the learned sit in long rows saying,
"Some A-s are not B-s, there exists a not B."
You'll have time to grow wise in their company.

MARKOS ARGENTARIOS

Don't pay any attention
To this synthetic spectre
Raving interchangeably
About the revolution
Of the exploited masses
And the diseased gyrations
Of his sensibilities.
He was a bride last night.

MARTIAL

Erotion rests here, in the
Hastening shadows, destroyed
By criminal fate in her
Sixth winter. You, whoever
You are, who rule over
This little field after me,
Pay your respects to her small
Ghost each year, that your hearth
May endure, and your family
Be safe, and only this stone,
Out in the fields, ever bring forth a tear.

MARTIAL

I send you a lock of hair
From an Arctic race, Lesbia,
So that you may know how much
More golden is your own.

MARTIAL

Since your marriage you have lost the look
Of a morose, inhibited wolf.
Perhaps your wife is reversible?

MARTIAL

Thais, why do you call me old
And garrulous? I am just
Experienced and smooth tongued.

MARTIAL

You are a stool pigeon and
A slanderer, a pimp and
A cheat, a pederast and
A troublemaker. I can't
Understand, Vacerra, why
You don't have more money.

MARTIAL

You are the most beautiful
Girl there ever was or will be.
And you are the vilest girl
There ever was or will be.
O Catulla, how I wish
You had less beauty or more shame.

MARTIAL

Down through the earth as a last gift,
Heliodora, I send you
My tears—tears of pain on a tomb
Already wet with weeping.
There was a time I wept for love
Longed for and love satisfied; now
I have only pain of love lost—
An empty gift to send you, dead.
O God, you were so beautiful,
So desirable. Death seized you,
Violated you like a flower
Smashed into dust. Let the earth
Which has borne us all, bear you,
Mourned by all, gently forever.

MELEAGROS

I swear by desire
I would rather hear
Your voice than the sound
Of Apollo's lyre.

MELEAGROS

What have you got to crow about,
Beating yourself with your red wings?
This hour is for final drowsy
Wantonries, not for your noisy
Virility. Go back to bed,
Or we will mourn this maidenhead
With a chicken dinner.

MELEAGROS

One deaf man went to law with
Another, before a judge
Who was deafer than either.
The first said, "He owes me five
Months' rent." The second said,
"He grinds it all night." The judge
Regarded them thoughtfully,
And said, "Now, boys, don't fight. She's
Your mother, you should both keep her."

NICHARKOS

Let us go into the temple
And look at the image of
Aphrodite, curiously
Wrought of gold. Polyarchis
Gave it, from the rich harvests
Of her own body's splendor.

NOSSIS

"Nothing is sweeter than love.
Every bliss takes second place.
Even honey I spit out of
My mouth." I, Nossis, say this,
"If any girl is unkissed
By love, she cannot tell what
Sort of flowers roses are."

NOSSIS

I have sworn ten thousand times
To make no more epigrams.
Every ass is my enemy now.
But when I look at your face,
The old sickness overcomes me.

PALLADAS

Let this life of worry
Pass by in silence, as
Silent as Time itself.
Live unknown, and so die.

PALLADAS

This is all the life there is.
It is good enough for me.
Worry won't make another,
Or make this one last longer.
The flesh of man wastes in time.
Today there's wine and dancing.
Today there's flowers and women.
We might as well enjoy them.
Tomorrow—nobody knows.

PALLADAS

We Greeks have fallen on evil
Days and fancy a dream is life.
Or is it we who are dead and seem
To live, or are we alive after
Life itself has departed?

PALLADAS

Don't tell me I'm getting gray,
That my eyes are red and bleared.
It's just love having a romp.
He kicks me where it hurts most,
Sticks arrows in me for fun,
Keeps me awake with lewd tales;
My loins are prematurely
Shriveled; my neck is scrawny;
I wane in a waxing fire.
If you would only relent—
I would grow plump at your touch,
And my hair turn black in a night.

PAULOS SILENTIARIOS

Eros has changed his quiver
For the fangs of Kerberos,
And I am hydrophobiac.
The sea smells of her body.
Her skirts rustle in the stream.
I go blind staggering drunk
With the very taste of wine
That calls back her sleep drugged lips.

PAULOS SILENTIARIOS

You're right, Lais' smile is sweet,
And the tears that drop from her
Fluttering eyelids are sweeter still.
Yesterday she leaned over me
And rested her head upon
My shoulder and sighed a long
Sigh. She wept as I kissed her
And tears fell from those dewy springs
And wet our mingled lips. And when
I asked her why she cried she
Said, "I am afraid you will
Leave me. You are all liars."

PAULOS SILENTIARIOS

Fornication is a filthy business,
The briefest form of lechery,
And the most boring, once you're satisfied.
So let's not rush blindly upon it,
Like cows in rut.
That's the way passion wilts
And the fire goes out.
But so and so, feasting without end,
Lie together kissing each other.
It's a lazy shameless thing,
Delights, has delighted, always will delight,
And never ends, but constantly begins again.

PETRONIUS

Good God, what a night that was,
The bed was so soft, and how we clung,
Burning together, lying this way and that,
Our uncontrollable passions
Flowing through our mouths.
If I could only die that way,
I'd say goodbye to the business of living.

PETRONIUS

I had just gone to bed
And begun to enjoy the first
Stillness of the night,
And sleep was slowly
Overcoming my eyes,
When savage Love
Jerked me up by the hair,
And threw me about,
And commanded me to stay up all night.
He said, "You are my slave,
The lover of a thousand girls.
Have you become so tough that you can lie here,
All alone and lonely?"
I jumped up barefoot and half dressed,
And ran off in all directions,
And got nowhere by any of them.
First I ran, and then I lingered,
And at last I was ashamed
To be wandering in the empty streets.
The voices of men,
The roar of traffic,
The songs of birds,
Even the barking of dogs,
Everything was still.
And me alone,
Afraid of my bed and sleep,
Ruled by a mighty lust.

PETRONIUS

That night will long delight us, Nealce,
That first cuddled you upon my breast,
The bed, and the image above it,
And the secret lamp by which you gave
Yourself, so softly, into my power.
For these, we can let age gain on us,
And enjoy the years which a little while
Will erase. It is fitting so
To prolong our love as we grow old,
And let what happened so suddenly,
Never suddenly stop.

PETRONIUS

Waking, my eyes, and in the night
My soul, seek you. Overcome
By my body, in my lonely bed,
I see you beside me, lying,
In the lying visions of sleep.
We would murder sleep
If you really came to me.

PETRONIUS

Why do you frown on me, you puritans,
And condemn the honesty of my latest poems?
Be thankful for fine writing
That makes you laugh instead of weep.
What people do, an honest tongue can talk about.
Do you know anybody who doesn't enjoy
Feasting and venery?
Who forbad my member to grow hot in a warm bed?
Father Epicurus himself commanded us
To become really sophisticated in this art.
Furthermore, he said this was the life of the gods.

PETRONIUS

Past fifty and cloyed at last,
Nikias, who loved to love,
Hangs up in the temple of
Kypris her sandals, her long
Uncoiled hair, her shining bronze
Mirror that never lied to her,
Her rich girdle, and the things
Men never mention. Here you can
See the whole panoply of love.

PHILETAS

Antikrates knew the stars
Better than Aratos, but
He couldn't cast his own
Horoscope. He said he didn't
Know if he was born under
The Ram, the Twins, or the Fish.
He should cast it in all three,
He is a whoremaster, a fool,
And a faggot.

PHILODEMOS

Death has torn ten years from us,
Xanthippe, since the day we met
And we had already lost
Thirty, and now grey hairs sprinkle
My head and maturity
Threatens me. But still I love
The sound of your singing voice,
And our thighs locked in a dance,
And my hungry heart still burns . . .
Or, to be brief about it,
I am crazy about you, Xanthippe.

PHILODEMOS

Hello. Hello. What's your name?
What's yours? You're too curious.
So are you. Have you got a date?
With anybody who likes me.
Do you want to go to dinner?
If you like. OK, how much?
You don't have to pay in advance.
That's odd. After you've slept with
Me, you can pay what you think
It's worth. Nothing wrong with that.
Where do you live, I'll call you.
Take it down. What time will you
Come? Whenever you say. Let's
Do it now. OK, walk ahead of me.

PHILODEMOS

Herakles' rebuttal was too much
For the thug who butted folks to death.
Your sophisticated responses
Have left me crippled, on the near side
Of middle age and midnight.

PHILODEMOS

In the middle of the night
I stole from my husband's bed
And came to you, soaked with rain.
And now, are we going to
Sit around, and not get down
To business, and not bill and coo,
And love like lovers ought to love?

PHILODEMOS

Philainion is short and
Quite black, and her hair crinkles
Like parsley, but her flesh is
Smooth as down and her voice sounds
More magical than the cestus.
She is always ready for
Anything, and often lets
Me have it free. I'll put up
With such a Philainion,
O golden Kypris, until
A better one is invented.

PHILODEMOS

Roses are already here,
Sosylos, and fresh peas,
And the first cut sprouts, and
The minnows that taste of
The surf, and salt soft cheese,
And the tender leaves of
Crinkly lettuces. But
Sosylos, we no longer
Go for walks on the beach
Or sit looking out at
The view, like we used to.
Antigenes and Bacchios
Were playing with us only
Yesterday, and today
We carried them to their graves.

PHILODEMOS

Sit down under the high crown
Of this pine, always sounding
In the steady West Wind, and
Here by the splashing current
Pan's pipe will entrance your
Spellbound eyelids.

PLATO

If Pythias has a customer,
I'll leave, but if she's sleeping alone,
For God's sake let me in a minute,
And tell her in my favor, that drunk
And through thieves, I came to her with
Only daring Love for my guide.

POSEIDIPPOS

You who visit in turn
Kypris and Kythera
And Miletus, and the
Beautiful Syrian
Plains, loud with horses' hooves,
Come now, graciously, to
Kallistion, who never
Turned a lover from her door.

POSEIDIPPOS

. . . about the cool water
the wind sounds through sprays
of apple, and from the quivering leaves
slumber pours down. . . .

SAPPHO

The moon has set,
And the Pleiades. It is
Midnight. Time passes.
I sleep alone.

SAPPHO

I fell in love with you, Atthis,
Long ago, when you were still
An ungainly little girl.

SAPPHO

This is the dust of Timias
Who went unmarried to the dark
Bedroom of Persephone. And
For her death all her girl friends cut
Their lovely hair with bright sharp bronze.

SAPPHO

I Lais, once an arrow
In the heart of all, am Lais
No longer, but a witness
To the harrying of the years.
I swear by Desire (and what
Is Desire but a swearword?),
Lais can no longer see
Lais in Lais herself.

SEKUNDOS

A great light was born in Athens when
Aristogeiton and Harmodios
Killed the tyrant Hipparchos.

SIMONIDES

Although your white bones waste in
The grave, I know the wild beasts
Still shudder, when they remember
The power of Lykas the
Huntress on great Pelion,
And far seen Ossa, and the
Lonely alps of Kithairon.

SIMONIDES

Stranger, when you come to
Lakedaimon, tell them we lie
Here, obedient to their will.

SIMONIDES

Here lies Anacreon,
An old man, a wine bibber,
And a lover of boys. His
Harp still sounds in silent
Acheron as he sings
Of the boys he left behind,
Megistheos who was so
Graceful, and that passionate
Thracian, Smerdies, and
Bathyllos and Euripyle.
The vine tendrils mingle with
His carven beard, and the white
Marble smells of wine and myrrh.

SIMONIDES, ANTIPATROS, AND OTHERS

Rivers level granite mountains,
Rains wash the figures from the sundial,
The plowshare wears thin in the furrow;
And on the fingers of the mighty,
The gold of authority is bright
With the glitter of attrition.

SULPICIUS LUPERCUS SERVASIUS, JR.

Remember now? Do you
Remember the time I
Told you the old saying,
"Nothing is as beautiful
As youth. Nothing is as
Fleeting as youth. The fastest
Bird of the air can't catch
Youth." And now look—your petals
Are all spilt on the earth.

THYMOKLES

Eumelos had a Maltese dog.
He called him Bull. He was the most
Loyal dog that ever lived.
His bark comes faintly up from Hell,
Lost on the night-bound roads.

TYMNES

Pass me the sweet earthenware jug,
Made of the earth that bore me,
The earth that someday I shall bear.

ZONAS

SELECTED ANN ARBOR PAPERBACKS
works of enduring merit

For a complete list of Ann Arbor Paperback titles write:

THE UNIVERSITY OF MICHIGAN PRESS / ANN ARBOR